WORDS
BETWEEN
DARKNESS & LIGHT

Poems by Una Kobrin

ORCHARD HOUSE PRESS
Nevada City, CA

Words Between Darkness and Light: Poems, by Una Kobrin.
Copyright © 2023 by Una Kobrin. All rights reserved.
Published by Orchard House Press.

Orchard House Press
unakobrin@gmail.com

Cover Design:
Una Kobrin

Cover Illustration:
The Omega Nebula or Swan Nebula in outer space.
Elements furnished by NASA

Editing:
Deborah Steinberg / Kathleen Fenton

Proofreading:
Jacquelyn Levy

Book Development and Production:
Naomi Rose

Book Design & Typesetting:
Margaret Copeland, Terragrafix

Printed in the United States of America

First printing 2023

ISBN: 979-8-9889291-0-9

Reader Praise for Words Between Darkness and Light

"*Words Between Darkness and Light* is not the typical book of poems you peruse and then store on a shelf. Through the years, I find myself astonished at their radiant beauty and wisdom, reaching again and again for them through seasons and cycles within the human soul and Nature. Una's poems are a prescient road map for the heart; its journey of joy and sorrow, wandering and wondering, remembering and reaching — the perceptive passion and power of a soul pilgrimage. *Words Between Darkness and Light* is a book not to leaf through but to live through. May you walk its pages with your heart."

— Patricia Kaminski, author, *Flowers That Heal*

"Una Kobrin's poems have been created from an inspired place, full of rich, beautiful imagery and a depth of feeling and insight. Her nature poems are extraordinary, the work of an experienced gardener and mystic, immersing us in a world of enchantment and wonder. Her poems are subtle, with often unexpected perspectives that reward multiple readings; a book to savor, like a fine wine."

— Ralph Dranow, author, *A New Life: Poems*; co-author with Daniel Marlin, *At Work on the Garments of Refuge*

"I have known and treasured Una's poems for many years. They have taken me to heights and depths, to places hidden in the soul, to moments of humor, wonder, illumination, empathy, self-realization. They are beautifully written and without affectation. This book is a gift!"

— Kathleen Fenton, artist

"Una Kobrin's poems let the reality outside ourselves open up what's great within. The gift is her unique voice, a blend of sensuality, beauty, and regular transcendental leaps that leave one in the pleasant grip of wonder."

— Eliot Schain, author, *The Distant Sound*

"With tenderness and humor, Una Kobrin's poems explore how the universe is contained in the smallest beings and experiences. This collection is a reminder to wake up to the wonder inherent in every moment, whether the moment is difficult, fleeting, sorrowful, exultant or mundane."

— Deborah K. Steinberg, editor, *Rivet: The Journal of Writing That Risks*

"Una Kobrin takes delight in the physical world with luxurious descriptions of all that she sets her eyes on. Her poems invite the reader to share in that pleasure and partake in the sly playfulness at work in her writing. "Awakened" opens with this seemingly matter-of-fact assertion: "I'm being watched / The wide-open eye of the moon / sees through my filmy curtain...." Kobrin reaches beyond the physical world as she contemplates its marriage to the spiritual, whether she is evoking the Sabbath or conjuring in imaginative detail the two grandmothers she never met. Readers are bound to enjoy accompanying this lively poet in her quest."

— Paula Friedman, author, *Undreaming Landscapes*

"Una Kobrin's nature poetry marries clear perception with insightful introspection. For example, her Madia poem demonstrates a very 'exact sensory imagination' (to use Goethe's term). The poem is a masterful integration of soulful images with clear observations that stay true to the actual phenomena of the plant, and true to her own inner experience. Through her skillfully wrought words, we are schooled in the artistic perception of the time-body of this plant, as it weaves through its diurnal cycle of closing and opening in response to the sun's movement. Then we are invited to re-create the Madia process as an inner centering experience. For those of us living in a culture of constant distraction and externalization, this is true soul medicine."

— Richard Katz, co-director, Flower Essence Society

"Una's poems draw vivid images of our human potentials and possibilities. They are an invitation to slow down and reimagine our personal relationship with Nature."

— Renee Wade, author, *The Living Earth Handbook*

To my daughter Rahel,
pearl of my heart

"All truths wait in all things."
— WALT WHITMAN

Contents

Acknowledgments

My deepest thanks to:

My original publisher, Naomi Rose, for her knowledge, deep listening, continuing support, and belief in my work.

My editors—Deborah Steinberg, who helped guide me through with valued comments, and Kathleen Fenton, whose sensitive listening, discernment, and sincere encouragement lifted me.

My proofreader, Jacqueline Levy, for her swift and astute reading and support.

My beloved family and friends, who have been feeding and prodding me with encouragement.

My teachers, everyone.

And most particularly, my dearest teachers Pir Vilayat Inayat Khan, Hazrat Inayat Khan, Rabbi Zalman Schachter, Rudolf Steiner, Pir Zia Inayat Khan, Dennis Klocek, and Faisal Muqaddam.

Foreword

*Poetry is a threshold — across which the groom carries
the bride from the outside to the inside — and the bride
brings the inside out, imbued with the inner wedded life.
This weaving in and out, knitting together relationships —
and it is all relationships with life, be it cloud or bird or tree,
family or friend or idea — and in some way join what feels
most alive and essential with the miracle of words.*

— UNA KOBRIN

I've been very fortunate to be on the inside track of this debut book of poems by Una Kobrin. As a long-time friend, I was blessed to be on the receiving end of her poems over a span of years, as they gradually made their way into the level of clarity and perfection that their author sought. Una has a remarkable intuitive acuity for finding the phrase, the word, the image, the feeling-tone to translate her vision of the world to readers who may not at the outset be familiar with that world. And it is a vision worth knowing — singular and interesting, enabling us to know ourselves and life more broadly, deeply, intimately.

Una's relationship to her land in Northern California, once heavily mine-stripped, has influenced the background and foreground of her work, and many of her poems. Her work on the land was informed and inspired by Rudolph Steiner's Biodynamic approach, which goes beyond organic methods to generate greater aliveness to a devitalized earth. Consequently, Una has not only restored the land but turned it into a lush paradise filled with gardens, ponds, sculptures and meditative places to be restored. She calls this alchemized land "Heartstone."

That the title she chose for this compilation of 96 poems is "Words Between Darkness and Light" is fitting not only for the poems that fill this book but also for someone dedicated to helping people find the light *in* the darkness, those unwanted, unloved aspects of ourselves that we tend to push away. This "disowning" of the painful parts of oneself is reflected in the poem, "The Avoided." Her poem "If Each" speaks to our darkness projected onto the world:

> "If each one of us ate one small grain of our darkness
> there wouldn't be so large a portion for the scapegoats
> to swallow."

The chapters of this book unfold describing aspects of light and darkness and our various relationships to it, beginning with Encounter: Threshold of Light and ending with Time: In Light of Time. In the chapter Kindred: Beings of Darkness and Light, Kobrin's poems draw from her life friendships and familial relations, which reveal the intricacies of relationship and the inner work toward redemption.

In the memorable poems on complex human relations such as "*Ishq*" (the Sufi word for Love), not only the inconsistencies and difficulties of a relationship are brought forward in poetic language, but also the growth and persistence of love despite the difficulties:

> "You opened my eyes with a crowbar,
> hugged me with vise grips…
> tried punching holes in my reason with a power drill…
> But beneath your ladder and hammer,
> I grasped your unbearably tender pomegranate-heart,
> leather-skinned heroism…"

Throughout the book, Una's spiritual perceptions permeate the text with remarkable heart and mind, from "Why We Need the Sabbath," to giving voice to the Divine Feminine in "Mother of Gestation," and the insightfully related parable about the Biblical Jonah, "Where Goodness is Found."

> "Still, Jonah was chosen
> not because he had become perfect
> and not for his constant faith
> but for God's faith in him,
> How else could we be released
> into the sea of life?"

May these poems between darkness and light release you beautifully into the sea of life.

— NAOMI ROSE

In addition to being publisher of the first edition of Words Between Darkness and Light *(Rose Press), Naomi Rose is a Book Developer & Creative Midwife.*

Prologue

Each poem, like a child, emerges uniquely. And like children some are intended while others are somewhat of a surprise. Whichever the case may be, aside from the rare poem that comes out complete in one uninterrupted emergence, poems, for me, are more of a labor and midwifing of an experience that develops throughout the process. Each one is a particular relationship reflecting some aspect of being, human or otherwise. Each respective examination potentially brings me closer to the essence of the other being, form or idea. My essence is in some way discovering and uncovering its essence, uniquely perceived and expressed through this/my individuality. The unique source of the other in some way potentially brings me closer to the Source.

This is an intimacy that requires my kindling and tending. It is a wedding of one individual consciousness with another consciousness, unearthing the common ground, finding the way Home. Each one of us who takes this on of course does this so very uniquely. And maybe in the sharing of our work, be it poetry, fiction, non-fiction, visual art or music, we might awaken something latent in the reader, viewer, listener that will be of value to them.

In art or work of any kind, we can distill the experience into process and product. There is malleability in both process and product. In poetry, the fluid mind and heart are the shaping forces. They are not only shaping but being shaped in the process, each moment uniquely impresses itself in the mix. Changing and editing is often on-going, as each time I reread a piece I am different and I may hear it in some new way. At some point, I need to stop and regard the earlier version of the self who wrote the poem 10 years before.

I realize the "I" as a uniquely formed, lively vessel through which Life/Spirit pervades. Ever-changing forces of Life are differently received and on-going. The particular color and mood of what information arrives interests me, and at the same time the shaping force within me is not always indifferent. The process in the moment is also a relationship between what has been/is and what is newly being and becoming. There can be a tussle. Resolution most often happens on the deeper level, the realm of changelessness. That is the Source that I seek to graze and feed from and, most hopefully, share with others. This underlying intention is not evident or even conscious in many poems, but as I reflect on the overall arc of my work, the impulse is toward growing unity while savoring the extraordinariness of each unique expression of the whole through words.

ENCOUNTERS

Threshold of Light

The Beloved Came

That evening the Beloved came,
and with sleight of hand
unfastened an old corset
I hadn't known I was wearing
anchored around my heart,
opening flood gates,
sending up wreckage of
shame and regret —
some mine, some others' —
burdens that barged,
never belonging but
docked there.

Each unhooking released a
binding of weights — one
unleashed a cry
of my mother
and my mother's mother and
the sounds of
her motherland, until
a strangling aah note
was freed.

Then each loosened lace let in
an eyelet of sky exposing
filmy layers — old images
fading transparent,
burning away all cover
until I was naked
in the light of night.

Awakened

I'm being watched.
The wide-open eye of the moon
sees through my filmy curtain,
pulls the cover off my sleep,
draws me to her hypnotic gaze.

I attempt to cobble dream wisps
into my night awakening,
but all that might be sensical
is incinerated in her white light —
absorbed into Her aliveness —

Her unhurried whirling dance
unveiling the naked darkness
disappearing and returning
in the thinnest veil
our eyes detect —
thread by thread exposing
her cloak of light.

Now in fullness
her mercurial pouring,
shimmering back
like a signaling lighthouse,
calling her story out of us
in rhythms of gaping time,
enchanting the rise and sway
of the ocean and each creature's
throbbing birth.

White Goddess
Rib of the Earth—
our awakened dream.

Water

Even before
I glimpse
your sparkling
tremble,
your nearness
meets me
in the air —

heady
sweetness
at the creek

or the river
tinctured with fish
and weathered moss,
or your brusque-briny
sea spray
upon our skin
soaking shore
edge into edgelessness,
enveloped in
your liquid flesh

reminding us
of our indissoluble
relationship.

Would we release you
from your piped servitude,
catch you in bowls
or pitchers,
lily ponds,
crystal vessels,
cupped hands —
allow you to spill out —
breathe and stretch
into your wide-eyed
reflections?

Handshake

A connecting place,
a small-scale embrace,
friendly but safe,
reading temperature,
motion and pressure.

"Shake my hand and be … one of us!"
"Nail the handshake for the perfect job."
"Put it there."
"Right here."

There is a warm squeeze, urging trust,
a bashful hand too timid to meet a palm,
the clammy hand we'd like to drop,
or the unrelenting fiery grip
and the one that ends before it begins,
limp, weightless fingers
like falling branches
or love stories folded in
a final moment's clutch.

And the shaky hand
that can barely hold a glass,
so wanting your contact,
apologizing for how she exists,
hoping you'll forgive her
but you don't know what for.

Who We Are

You think you are skin, blood,
organ meat, grey matter,
there is convincing evidence —
but not whole truth.

That is only a raincoat
and your skin-tight genes,
as if they were the last word.

Beneath them —
insulated underwear, and
under that
girdles, straps and bindings,
a leopard-skin loincloth,
and still more layers
back of the closet.

Take off the merit badges,
fraying blue ribbons,
letters after your name
worn on paper.

Take away your holdings,
bonds and stocks,
all valuables or
pride of poverty,
the leg up or step down
of pedigree or heredity,
and do not forget associations.

Then, if you want a real introduction,
"Undress completely from yourself." *

*Jalāl ad-Dīn Rumi, from *The Little Book of Life*

Light a Candle

Light a candle,
Bring it within.

This flame is halo enough
to waken the huddled darkness —
black silhouettes frozen in time.
Watch their edges fidget
as they thaw and arouse,
awaiting your discovery.

They are overstayed guests
wanting one thing or another.
Shine this light upon them —
see who's who,
each one speaks
a different tongue,
so listen carefully, to each.

What they want is you.
Step bravely into
their shadowy feet,
enter the shape of their flesh,
listen for the trail of their longing,
what you have been carrying.

If you give them
what is inside their asking,
you will receive.

They may go, vacate.

What remains?

An open window,
a clearing,
new fields of fresh life
to stretch, roam,
and climb as pulsations
of a flame.

The Arrangement

The glass cylinder, half filled with water,
disappears beneath a woody bouquet,
exposing her romance with the spare
beauty of the day.

Stray branches dangle
hints of sanguine and saffron,
pale gold seed-heads
frame the lacing space of stillness.

Amid her quiet seasonal picks —
a singular rose holds me,
a consummation
from centuries of roses
culled by absorbed rosarians
in their delicate passion.

Fugitive colors of damask pink,
tinted claret and lapis
make their home in its
unwinding whorl of petals.

Octaves of fragrance
spiral back to the first
imagination of roseness,
to carry us into winter's restraint.

SEASONS

Movement of Darkness and Light

Anamnesis*

Curious how the breaking bud
brings a known surprise,
a recollection drawn from us
like a newborn infant,
still covered in cosmic milk,
experiencing the first
startling freedom of the air,
steering our senses
to fragrance upon fragrance —
earth breath, green rain,
butter-cupped meadows.

Spring is the first thought remembrance —
the just-birthed idea we already know.
It is not only crocus and plum blossoms awakening
but a living picture of the earth beginning again,
never lost but breathed back
into our communal resurrection.

* The remembering of things from a supposed previous existence.

Too Soon Spring

Spring has become pink too soon,
waking underground longings,
cutting short the hidden work
of winter's deep transmission,
coaxing buds out of sleep
to sprout and dangle rosy promises
which die in night's chill.

Like lifting the sacred skirts
of budding girls,
petals pulled open from
the holy shrine to steal
the spring out of them,
robbing them of their season's
inner stirring warmth,
a cruelty to nature's covenant.

The grace of ripening, of Earth's
holding back seed and root
while the plans of the cosmos
imprint star-signed maps,
cannot be hurried along
without cost.

Impatience with time—
growing things unnaturally,
forcing cows to ever give milk,
chickens to always lay,
and girls to be women —
denying the winter womb —
concocts a forever Spring,
a truly never Spring.

After the Rain

If you stay dry and undercover
you'll miss the newly washed
world outside.

You can still catch remains
of the potent draft —
heavenly dew hanging in the air,
too light to have
fallen with the rain.

And the wind's sweet breath
is here too,
come from many worlds away,
muttering with a distant tongue,
murmuring the finest fragments
of the first words.

Mingle with this good company,
be doused clean with
resurrected water,
get baptized in this instant.

Breathe in the pristine ether
that has journeyed for
countless years,
been spun by planets,
pulled by comets,
lit by stars —
refashioned light.

If you close your eyes,
drink in slowly
the lingering water,
you might taste Jupiter.

May Rain 1

This rain has magnified the beauty of the earth
like a giant lens laid on it.
Its watery reflection clears my burdened head
flooded by the force and might of spring —
and the weed work that it brings,
slowing my steps, as walking through water would.

The earth's body fragrances seduce me.
Each scene stops me in my tracks
and I stand new as a spring bud.

May Rain 2

The rain's countless kisses have left love jewels—
magnifying orbs heightening our senses,
bejeweling the blossoms, as if they needed ornamentation.
No, these drops are intoxicating liquid,
the blossoms are drunk, they can't keep their heads up.

This soaking made a perfect bed for wildflower seeds,
I'll scatter them on this new wine —plant these living prayers.

California Summer

These days the sun hits hard,
stripping the green pliancy
from thin-reaching grasses.

We pray for heavy clouds
only to see chem trails
and begin to count the days
when a miracle-storm might come.

But then the plums plump purple
and you can taste the last rain
sweetened inside them

Summer Overcast

A dim slow sea drifts above the pines,
dampening the sun's fire,
sheltering with its lofty comforter
of clouds stretched across the sky.

A softening happens,
quelling the harsh glare of day,
finespun air weaves moist around us,
clenching bodies ease their hold.

Pores begin to catch their breath,
lips part in quiet awe, edges unfix,
the overcast begins roaming inside us,
breath by breath we are mingled.

The arid soaks, then spills
with mist into a watercolor
atmosphere inside us —
dark and light flare
into unbroken veils of color.

This Autumn Day

This autumn day's spacious wrapping —
an airy nest of wide-reaching branches,
a lookout for viewing the beautiful
procession of death.

Who will be the first to go?
The elder, leaves barely holding on,
soon to be a skeleton of itself?
The burning bush, bleeding a
puddle of scarlet.
The dogwood flushed in viewing.

Each takes its turn in this
tenuous instant before
the severity to come.
Then the tender breeze —

The torch of Maximillian sunflowers
dims, electric blue statice prostrates,
while lumens of redbud leaves
drop as fallen stars.

This place, this day and I are lovers,
engaged in a last glance.

Winter Solstice

You, chosen of the darkness,
ignored during bright flowery hours,
now snugly contracted, content
with the smaller window of day,
drawing us farther into your
dimming mine —

then, out of time's underside —
the sun turns a corner,
slits open the trapdoor,
looks you square in your mood.

What will become of you now?

After you've rubbed the moon's sheen
from your nocturnal eyes, sensing
that gritty intrusion from the thieving light,
you are a bear stolen from winter,
a heart, grave-robbed.

Is it all so bad?

You say shadow is where you poke at the inscrutable,
sleuthing glimmers beneath your opaque cape,
pulling out creations from the black hat of night,
with a magician's mind and a baker's hands
or penetrate hidden passages to the other side.

The Hand of Winter

At dew point,
tiny fingers of frost
rise from the ground,
heaving up the earth's
coarse sediment,
bringing above what was
unseen in summer's high cover.

Without winter's closer light,
crystal touch and skeletonized
unveiling, a hidden world
might go unnoticed.

Winter lays its hand
on us too, our crystalline
blood-salt and bones
of hardened light
are raised within us.

An inner sun rises
to kindle soul tending —
a fiery friction sparks
like flint inside —
exposing darkest caverns,
deep craggy turns lure,
floors collapse beneath us.

Out of death-like stillness,
coarse deposits crumble
exposing gold-veined tracks,
drawing us down to our mother lode.

Beneath glow embers,
diamond cathedrals of light
lay hidden and waiting,
under the foot of our knowing.

UNEARTHING

Excavating the Light

"Language Is Fossil Poetry"[*]

Pick up a word or phrase
that's been dropped.
Chip away at it.

Loosen the debris.
Somewhere within it
remains a remnant of
what was once alive,
now held together with clay and stone,
life so old we cannot name it.

A hidden trace, impression,
existence frozen,
a gesture once animate —
in dance, chant, drum beat —
chiseled or blown with color.

These leavings, vestiges of voice,
give testimony of a time
when the air was fresh
with Holy Breath
and words were living,
recognized from fluid
scriptures —bestowed upon
all creatures, as Adam did.

Poetry that is prayer
plants living words
back into the air.

*Title from Ralph Waldo Emerson.

Burnt Breadcrumbs

Burnt breadcrumbs speckle rose petals,
become bedfellows
in a casket for compost.
Bits of eggshell and apple core,
which would never rub up against
one another in their native homes,
find common ground in death.

All share in mutual decomposition,
all lose form, fall apart
over-ripened, rotting and molding.

Earthly undertakers prepare the remains,
cooled leftovers heat up in a second offering —
many-legged and no-legged creatures
prepare for tiniest soil life to feast upon.

It is not an instant miracle,
but the rapt engagement of
the less visible world,
each perfectly made to imbibe
and ingest its particular provisions,
taking part in the good work.

Earth, air, warmth and water
join in the alchemy
of the great metamorphosis —
the putrid becoming purified —
the dead enlivened — we walk on it,
transubstantiation beneath our feet.

Watching this loaf of warming compost,
I wonder, does the Holy One watch us
in a similar way, patiently waiting
for the life within us
to be carefully worked over —
digested into fertile purpose?

The Avoided

Friend,
what if your pain
was a gathering place
for the too many
sorry events of your life —
unwanted memories
all pressed together,
held in an airless train,
stopped dead on its tracks —
mouth gagged,
no water or bread,
forced into silence —
walled in, ignored
and abandoned?

Go there now,
break through
the barricade!

Find the sorrow
in this petrified place
take its hand,
move it gently,
offer support
to its naked bones.

Moisten the fused-dry lips
with thawing tears.
Ask what is hiding there?
Kindly coax the secret dread.
Place yourself at its service,
offer today's fresh fruit.
Give it time to chew.

Then, walk it through
the broken wall into the open air.

Be patient—it may move slowly.

Now see through its eyes—
a new world.

It may stare out in wonder.
It might smile, laugh, cry.

Don't drop its bony hand,
put it to your cheek
and ask yourself,
"Is this what I was afraid of?"

Weeding

Like a primate mother
about to preen her young,
I seize the well-advantaged
intruders,
better equipped for piercing
the tight-fisted earth
than the fine-haired roots
of my cultivated delicacies.

But I am a contender
on this small fragment of the world,
my fingers know the rooting ways
of the unbidden oxalis —
how to pull the deep-threaded
bindweed, and yank out
the piercing foxtails hidden
in the sharp unruly grasses.

Still, these formidable foes
have won my respect
as innovative survivalists —
furthering earth's blossoming.

What they are and what they do
for a living is one continuous
ever-changing perfect response,
even in death by my hand.

And long after my weeding hands
lay upon my chest beneath the ground
and my memorial flowers withered,
abiding weeds will cover my bony remains.

The Wood Pile

The one who piled this wood
left a bit of biography here,
each log and branch
placed with close attention,
as if the great fallen cedar
and woodsman spoke
to each other in a silent
language of form,
its gestures guiding him
in motionless grace —
the turns of its limbs,
shaped by its reach to the sun
and succumbing to the wind —
now point to where
its branches might be laid
among its once-mighty roots,
that anchored in the earth
all its many years.

When it was sawn and falling —
first in a long slow-motion,
then sped up by gravity —
cracking open the wooded stillness
with its own thunder,

did the earth pause?

Severed, its body was reclaimed
for yet another purpose,
carved by human hands,
piled into a heap of sawn limbs
sized for the stove, but left there.

I imagine the one who found
the random mound
repositioning each wizened branch
like a petal of a flower, as if

arranging for a sacred funeral pyre
with contemplative regard
and an ordered beauty,
grown out from heartwood,
like the living tree itself.

Watched

Being seen
through a one-way window
violates our privacy.

But imagine
watching the viewers,
knowing their cronies,
hearing their plans,
being privy to what's hidden.

Everyone wired,
knowing everyone's business,
no place to hide.

All plots,
ill intentions
conspiracies,
secret codes,
political bribes,
sins at the pulpit,
plain as day.

Likewise,
dogged teachers,
champions of nature,
protectors of truth,
everyday heroism,
everywhere kindnesses,
as visible as violence.

To be moral would be practical,
unsurprising, usual
courtesy and goodwill familiar.

Now imagine
there are invisible ones,
watching from the other side,

wise way-showers right here
but unseen, unsolicited,
wanting to assist,
to offer benevolent counsel.
They have no voices,
no bodies to perform their acts of grace,
patiently waiting behind a one-way view.

THE FIELD

Field of Light

Moon Math

From an almost invisible fraction
to full orb —
so simple a geometry —
lit up on the blackboard sky
for perpetual beginners
viewing and reviewing —
the same, ever-changing lesson
lest we forget —
our common denominator —
we are each a part of the whole,
our primary equation —
so clear, so simple
and yet we keep it up in the sky.

Space

Space, the maiden presence
holding the first waters apart —
holds us — our turning earth,
without muscle or weight:
growing skyscrapers and sequoias,
raising dust and flying seeds,
embracing the loft of levity
and the ballast of gravity—
is scarcely nothingness.

In the midst of all places:
the solemn stretch of prairie,
hovering over the mountains,
bearing the many moods of clouds,
mingling pine, oak and fungal fragrances
throughout the forest.

Endlessness of the universe —
nearby, around us, here —
narrowly living within the atom,
making room for every individuality
and semblance to spin its ways.

Without it, there would be no separation —
no margins, or no membranes, no forms.
Organs would merge, planets would collide.

Benignly, spaciousness is here within us —
our bodies, more space than flesh.

Mother of Gestation

Unnoticed,
in the background,
too immense to consider,
too distant from the moment,
even though we are ever inside Her.

She who houses the nebulae above,
the earthly cities below.

Consort to the colossal plumes
of God's imaginative fire,
Her immense organs of creation
incubate cosmic life,
nurse celestial eggs,
spanning degrees from frigid to torrid,
guarded in her commodious womb,
swaddled with shimmering veils of light,
while stirring flaring seeds
into starry buds.

Within Her undulating skirts
swirl the fiery turns of planets,
stars gathering into
bouquets of galaxies.

Each one of us — a child-star
of Her unfathomable body.

What First

Has Light fallen from Love or
Love fallen from Light or
Has Light risen from Love or
Love risen from Light?

Were they the First Separation or
The First Wedding?

Beyond

I'll be an ancient lady,
my mind — star dust in space.
I'll wander far beyond the unknown
where forgetting has its place
and fear is dropped like an underskirt
released in the naked night
I'll soar to visit formless friends —
we'll know each other's light.

Break Out

Break out of your mind!
Wander into the unknown,
don't fear getting lost,
the Guide has left us love crumbs
to follow all the way home.

Of the Blue

Can our hearts be large enough oceans to hold
the love that comes from the sky?

Can we bear its serenity — flooding us with stillness
in its free embrace?

Can we envision all that has been extinguished, stirred
and newly lit up into luminous blue?

Can we, even if briefly, dwell in this in-between place —
where life dust mingles in its twilight of matter?

Can we imagine its boundless province to forever be in the
background as worlds spin and unravel their stories
again and again?

Can we fathom its azure veil of protection
shielding us from the unendurable face of God?

CREATURES

Legged Light

Mayflies Mating in June

The lifespan of an adult mayfly can vary from just 30 minutes
to one day, depending on the species. The primary function
of the adult is reproduction; the mouthparts are vestigial, and
the digestive system is filled with air.

No dark secret rendezvous,
hiding beneath a table or
dim corner-getaway,
the light by my entry door,
your spot for romancing.

My hand turns the key,
I take a voyeur's glance
from the corner of my eye.

As I enter the house,
you tumble through my doorway
ecstatically somersaulting in the air,
ignorant of the limits of human doors.

What could distract your rhapsodic dance?
Not I.
My fixed eyes are of no consequence,
modesty an absurd fabrication of civilization,
a dried-out cobweb,
not phasing your uninterruptible wedlock,
held in place by filament legs,
anteriors fixed and fueling.

What have great lovers throughout time
over you?
Indeed, love is all you live for —
your food, survival, your raison d'être.

So, gorge yourselves, suck each sweet moment dry.
What higher truth or nobler purpose
than to love and die for family, for specie,
for existence?

You are the pulsations of gypsy violins,
a signature of Zen brevity,
first and last kiss of a silent motion picture.

At last, exhaustion slows your tandem skydive,
pausing vertically, end to end
(her wings horizontal, his slightly raised).
Together an anchor in space
taking a gentle love doze.
Have you come to the end?
I wait in wonder.

Then a stir, a quickening —
your emptied passion is renewed —
in one gossamer thought
you arise as if a delicate wind curled
through my window,
raising you both in a rapture —
soaring amidst rare sparkling ethers,
lifting ceiling above cathedral height,
transcending even the lightness of angels.

Big Grey

His serpentine lean against you
was an unsteadying force of affection,
a grey lion in the kitchen
pacing his territory,
pushing the frontier
of forbidden doorways,
leaping onto tables
and counters,
stalking plates for
the morning's eggs
or remains from dinner.

This time when I visited,
he was a withered version
of that once-unruly grace,
his shape inelegant.
Age had gnawed his body
leaving little flesh,
pliancy hardened
and tentative,
his obedient coat raised
as if in fear.

Those inscrutable tiger eyes
had become burrows
his senses crawled into.

Once-forbidden places were
his to lodge, now that the
wildness was out of him.
Now he tracked for warmth
and her love softened for him,
without limit.

Ode to Tom

Who but you, a blue head
narrowly rising, a nod to the sky,
spewing that fiery volcanic wattle
above your bronze body-mount.

You've made it through winter,
survived predators
and the Thanksgiving knife
and now it's your rite of spring,

tail raying out in a succession
of extravagant amber plumage —
impersonating the sun —
in that strut-fluttering fan dance —
astonishing the hens.

"Here I am!"

And leaving your "here I was"
here and there,
so that we never miss a trace
of your always startling presence.

Things Great and Small

Minute as they are,
ordinary and startling,
sometimes looking like moving ground
filing over landscapes
unimaginable to our eyes,
their tireless industry —
elegantly wireless —
guiding labyrinthian
navigation routes.

When comrades die, they keep vigil,
carry on like brown-hooded Franciscan monks
forged to their mission, carrying
the crumbs of survival, with strength
that dwarfs Goliath's —
if human, would be heroes.

My need to end their in-house invasion,
to remove them — wipe them away,
stirs up the still, minute voice in me.

With every wipe and spray
I think of the Mighty Hand, cleaning up
Sodom and Gomorrah —
but these are instinctive innocents,
not sinners.

Killing them as if they were
lifeless dark specks on my counter,
from a Buddhist perspective
would further suffering,
while Hindus might advise
fearlessness when killing enemies
(death being an illusion).

This contemplative pause
is a pebble in my center,
a dubious privilege
of being human.

The Quick Grey Squirrel ...

Widely awake
to early morning solitude,

he silently imbibes from
sprinkler-fed puddle —

nose tracking
the residue of scat

speed-reads
the turkey chronicles

left along the walkway,
responding to each syllable,

punctuating with his tail
of prideful smoke.

Then hastens onto
his next course.

Where will it be,
up the tree or underground?

As above, so *buried* below.

Nesting

I'd like to be a nest,
long enough to receive an arrival:

I

I imagine my expectant robin
locating a fitting spot
to piece me together —
in a hidden crotch
of a lofty maple tree.

Drawing feathers in,
she goes about her art,
teasing out dry grasses,
pulling sedges, gathering
pliant twigs from forest trove.

Threads of tinsel from a half-buried
Christmas tree are woven in
to enchant the coming babes
while she's out winning worms.

While I am woofed and wefted,
entwined as a homespun wreath,
her doting helpmate maintains provisions.
With their mouthfuls of mud,
I am mortared.

Wickerwork done,
I am a timely basket fit
to hold her precious bounty.

II

At last, she rests
her soft orange breast
now burrowed into
this berth of her making.

Though I'm fashioned
from earth's dead matter,
her living spirit fills me with
pulsing warmth.

I hold her patient presence
as we await the coming.

> III

A trembling begins —
her grasping innards
strain to expel a form
whose beauty is wrought
by the hollow which holds it,
tapered with a slowing elegance
that midwifes its release.

Her stoic delivery of
these ordinary miracles —
three perfect sky-blue eggs —
leaves the gentle weight
of heaven inside me.

With warming wings
she swaddles her cerulean jewels.
Within each rests a milky sun
and dawning baby bird.

> IV

Days of tending pass —
each fleshy nebula ripening
into avian form — airship eyes,
wing buds, feather-hairs —
their firming beaks press
cramped capsules.

Faint percussive sounds
vibrate inside — tapping,
cracking, a long unzipping
opens the seal —
hatchlings tumble out
into the vast sky-world.

V

While mother takes her
frequent flights to sustain
their ravenous chirps —
I keep them steady
in their place until

the heightened moment
when their deepest hunger
is quickened — strength
and daring springs
their fledgling legs,
wings unfurl like flames —
in the heart-soaring thrill
of their first flight.

Now an empty nest —
I remain their launching pad.

Cricket

I room with a cricket.
His taut spring-loaded body
occupies little space.

In daytime, he's reserved,
withdrawn. In the evening,
he's a troubadour belting
pulsating love songs.

Although I'm not his first choice,
I'm contented to be a second,
listening to his broken croons.

When I Was a Minnow

Swimming in the pocket of my mother's belly
and when I emerged, love was never still.

Encircling her, brushing against her
but never in her firm grasp nor she in mine.

Love has been that — silken-moist,
sometimes rough-scaled, slither—
whether holding or being held,
even when close and still as sea depths,
the slick wet quicksilver
never stopping in time,
each moment a slippery minnow.

Our flipping — growing out of ourselves —
unceasingly until we release —
break out from our net
into the watery web,
embraced by the transparent sea,
waters passing through,
swimming the unbroken life.

The Rooster of Molokai

Before the first bloom of dawn
the old early-riser broke out again
with his ragged old crow — enough to start
the neighbor cocks (maybe too groggy
to notice the darkness)
flapping after that sound tag.

Perhaps this sentinel, like Don Quixote,
was seeing things — a glimmer from a Great Lighthouse,
maybe he was blind and awakened by an inner sun rising
to guide him to his resting place and set off an earlier day.

The next morning I overslept — silence blurred the day.
Imagining his fate paused my breath.
Had neighbors or tourists groused
about his predawn trumpeting,
awakening them at an ungodly hour?

Had the farmer heard those complaints one too many
times and thought,

"Maybe it's time for our faithful old bird to go,
have the wife make him into a stew. Invite the family and
complaining neighbors for dinner."

I wondered if that Chanticleer's well-played throat
would be tough or tenderized by all the dutiful mornings
of his heart-piercing arousals.

Pigeons of the City

So you're not a songbird,
more a janitor in the subway,
a low-down beggar on Broadway.

Few birders pull out binoculars
to watch you up close.

And your diet!
Who'd want to try it?
What would a taxidermist find
inside?

You're hardly prized or preserved
by hot-shot hunters.

But you're not squealing, dive bombing
or complaining about your lot.
And frankly, there's something
endearing in your coo.

So what if you're not one of the colorful ones?
Your serviceable feathers of flannel grey
suit you with distinguished subtlety.

Those penetrating yellow, blood-shot eyes
elicit a certain sympathy,
but your iridescent ruff of amethyst and jade
remains your visible allotment from heaven,
family jewels of the disregarded angels.

A Wag of Light

Her back-and-forth dashing
on the runway is not for show
but a throwback from a comet,
now unleashed in a current of joy

running between her territorial
ground and boundless air
charged above her,

breaking through
all leashes with
mindless play

while we stand in
the dust of her flurry,
short of words,
viewing fervent life.

She waits by my feet
in bursting stillness,
but for ticking tail.

How can I not take notice,
bow down to pet
and caress her
aimless dark curls,
as she serpentines
around my arm,
looking up with
beseeching eyes,
and articulate bark?

"Don't you get it?
This is what matters"

As a Bird

Like a baby sparrow
lifting her head,
mouth hinged open
in expectation of
a lively morsel
from her mother,
I lift my chin
open my mouth,
praise your name
and so I am fed.

KINDRED

Beings of Darkness and Light

What She Had
(for NHHN)

There were no articles
of particular value but to her,
no close brushes with fame,
no beautiful garments
but how she regarded them,
no letters after her name,
no plaques in her honor,
no great recipes,
no prominent awards,
no captivating features
except her sincere eyes,
two drops of the still ocean

and what she walked with, slowly,
what came from her nose-curling smile,
her modest veil of tenderness,
her love's welcoming generosity,
the hum of her cherishing
and gentle affirmation in her speech,
were the sum of her gifts —

And her diligently wrought work,
sewn with embroidered words
and rose petals.

My Grandmothers Sang

Everything in the kitchen
makes a noise —
a clatter of pans sets off a tone.

Warming leftovers,
I become a vibrating rod
sending out a familiar
chord into another time,
worlds away.

A soundless tune
echoes back
to my far-reaching
innermost ear —
an almost humming —
stirring me into musing
on my grandmothers.

The pressed violets,
on album pages fading away.

I knew one of them little
and the other not at all,
but this I know:
both had a love of singing.

PRELUDE

While quite young,
Lena was swept away
by a charming suitor,
married, and left behind
in a foreign country
as he ventured off to America
with a promise to send for her
after he found work
and funds for her voyage.

"My girl, my bride!
Jump in my boat
I'll take you beyond the seas
and the mountains,
Over two hundred miles,
Over the forests.
You won't hear, my girl,
Your mother's cries,
Your father's weeps;
You won't hear, my girl,
Your sisters' singing
Your brothers' dancing."
"My boy — my husband!
Where will I put my wreaths?"[1]

Some months later, on steerage,
led by her father's hand,
she arrived in the New World
on a low note of that fallen love,
with little more than girlhood melodies
to rub against the hope in her purse.

"Oh, my heart, what are you thinking of?
My violet, why don't you speak?
Rare is the wheat, rare
In which there isn't a knot,
Rare is the love
In which there isn't a fault,
More beautiful, better than myself.
O, my heart will not find
O, my heart will not find...."[2]

Rosa, my other grandmother,
followed her older sister, whose marriage
and getaway opened a path for her,
leaving homeland and loved ones,
with her few treasured possessions,
and the skills remembered in her hands.

"Adieu, my little treasure, I am now leaving this place
Unwillingly, out of must, I don't know what to do.
But I still believe that one day I will return
One way or another, I will love you as long as I live.
You know, my rose, when, even if not that often,
I used to play with you, even if not that often.
My blood still boils for you,
especially when wine ignites it."[3]

Rosa's dream, to be a singer,
to perform on the stage,
was stillborn — an impropriety
for a woman in her world.

"Don't look for me where birds sing.
You will not find me there, my beloved.
I am a slave where chains ring,
There is my resting place.
The sadness and the worries
Should go away with past dark years.
Laugh right in the wind's face...." 4

After a convenient marriage,
her voice was reserved
for the small kitchen audience —
stirring notes into goulash and paprikas
or intoning patterns while tatting lace.

Lena's singing, also, most always,
accompanied her chores — tunes
lifting the girlhood from her heart.
While baking, she was asked,

"What is this you're making?"
She replied,
"I put in only what's good,
so what could be bad?"

"Why should I be upset?
This existence is a song,
Hey, Yidl, fidl, shmidl —
This life is a joke." 5

INTERLUDE

A sad joke on each.

Did you think you'd left the colorless landscape?
Did you think you'd escaped the continent of grief?
Did you think you'd come to the new promised land,
sheltered beneath Lady Liberty's reach?

Still wearing your handed-down apron of silence,
what you could do was quell mistranslations,
change the volume, alter some lyrics or tone,
ease hardened throats with medicine melodies,
pull up *nigunim* of forbidden prayers.

Sing out rhythms to rouse lifeblood and backbone,
to catch stray *kinder*, lighten armloads of washing,
liven fingers to bread weave, pull threads to make ends meet
and keep yourselves tethered from routine's oblivion.

Sing songs that rise like a cake wafting fragrance,
leavening the flattening iron of the day.

BRIDGE

Grandmothers,
you don't know me, not really,
nor do I really know you, but
your white hairs thread into mine,
I raise you with the flesh of imagination.

Come use my eyes and ears — re-enter time —
this present, far from your long journey here —
to our still-fledgling refuge for freedom —
your feet met this soil, trudged its uneven roads.

Those steps grew to strides, and the yeast of your hope
ferments in ways unimaginable, recasting dreams.
All that you carried and earned has been furthered
and given new shape through voices of offspring.

And freedom is reforming in unknowable ways.

CODA

Now, I sing my song to my Grandmothers —
a silent song, without words or close,
that I might meet them someday in a subtler field —
where there is no up nor down nor limit
but a homeland of sound
where the soul's source resounds,
from which we have all come
and to which they have gone.

And now they live without end in that song.

[1-5] Excerpts from folk songs of their homelands.

Red Shoes

When my granddaughter Goldie first chose shoes,
the shoes she chose were red.

When I was young,
I had a pair of red shoes too.
They weren't for dancing—
blood-red leather,
exposed tongue, crowned
with a well-turned knot,
a hint of my heart,
tanned for my foot.

My mother had taken me
downtown shopping
for new shoes,
it was getting late
that hot summer's day,
when we settled on these—
I, for their ruddy swag,
she, for their cut price.

"How do they feel?" she asked.
"Okay," in cramped voice,
half-defying my discomfort.

I sensed they were more fitting
of my craved-for life than my feet.
I held hope that time would soften
the rubbing counters that blistered my heel.

I put them on in the subway,
holding onto the train pole.
I swayed that urban dance in them,
so they could never be returned.

Mary Jane's Light

Describing her light is impossible,
to think of her dead is unthinkable.

Back to her light — I'll attempt it:

Rarely still or even flickering,
it might dart or meander
around a group, or get settled,
sometimes column-like,
when she was speaking.

With her young grandson —
listening intently or story-telling —
she spoke in blossoms of light,
he moved them all over,
she held onto their stems.
If he fell into a tantrum
she became a green horizontal beam.

Her dead-heading roses in the garden
sent out sparks of those conversations,
inviting lady bugs, praying mantis,
nature spirits and gnomes,
young folk often trailing behind.

When inner beasts took residence
in her body, encroaching on her sight
and scattering tumors,
she drew light inside herself,
begging understanding
of what invited them.

Igniting her will, she resolved
"More art, more love "—
so she made time elastic —
awakening at wee hours,
stretching night, heightening day

with her own breaking dawn —
timed for a fluid freedom,
to create vivid soul collages,
which friends used to wallpaper
her coffin.

We formed a crescent moon
at the foot of her death bed,
where her daughter had been born.
She lay looking at us all,
wryly remarking,
"I don't see any tears."

If I'd not been with others
and half in a trance,
if I'd been solo beside her,
to gently lift her to my chest,
replace her gently to her pillow,
gaze into her dimming eyes
to tell her,

"Even your twilight is bright enough
to dry our tears."

After dark, a fox yowled
outside her window.

When she left her spare body,
weightless without the flesh of her spirit,
I would not have known her,
not without her smile,
which revealed her
as a godchild of the sun.

But now among the dearest past,
she has preciously tricked death —
love rose from her ashes.

Tantrums

I had them as a child
and was asked, "What is it?
What's the matter? Tell me."

My best recollection is —
a storm inside.

From an atmosphere
of unbounded light and
liveliest peace,
shimmering in color,
suddenly that all shifted …

I was exiled, contracted
into the tiniest form
plunged into a watery pouch,
rolling currents moving me —
growing among sounds —
massaging voices,
buzzing drones, and thuds —
then to be squeezed through
a narrowing passageway,
pulled head first —
out into space.

Intense glaring light,
filled with the weight of air —
cold then warmth.

All to come here.

Being in form, any form
sent a quiver in me.
After a time,
I cradled into it,
to later meet with
courtyards of concrete,

stories of gray,
a prevailing mood of gloom —
occasionally clouds parted
a sunny blink of humor —
then returning to turbulence
and energy collisions.

Perhaps less disturbing to others,
but my thin membrane
shuddered while high and low
pressures converged —
when my skin could no longer contain —
I stormed.

Words blew away in that wind.

Beyond Genetics

When I think of my dead parents,
I think, "I don't think of them enough."
Like the never-enough calls to my mother
ending with a hollow in my throat.

Then I touch my father's socks
in my sock drawer
or my mother's bifocals
on my nightstand,
and a lock is released—
from a safe in my chest
which held an ice-stone
melting into warmth.

And when I see the circles
under my eyes,
I think of how little sleep
my father got
or the lump on my arm that arose
at the exact place as my mother's,
I touch into memory recorded
in a more lasting way
than my fugitive thoughts
or judgments —

How I missed the mark,
how it would have been so easy
to thank them more —
but for our mined-barricades
it might have been more plain.

Yesterday, I recalled my father's
tennis elbow (though he never
played tennis, nor do I),
but each pull and flame
of my elbow reminds me
of his never-missed work,

and my mother, who daily
stretched her fiber.
I can be sympathetic in my body.

Sometimes I imagine them
being entirely different people
if they had been sincerely
appreciated by another.
That could have been me.

I grieve them in my body,
and somehow
in that fleshly double-take,
in some way we are redeemed
and somewhere, some when,
we are new to one another.

Mother, Child

MOTHER

Her face as familiar as the sky
Her touch second-nature
Her skin your skin
Her voice the one you turned to
Her smile the warmth of your world.
She loved you as no other
Hurt you as no other
and long after her warmth, like smoke,
passes into the periphery
and the first-hand pains
fade to the horizon
All that was in the repertory
of her touch is held in an old photo

You take in the breath of the world
and see out into the landscape differently
And you love her as you love the sunset

CHILD

Her face as startling as creation
Her perfect fingers orbiting
to feel the new world
Her closeness as pliant and deep
as the marrow of your bones
Her breath miraculous as life
Her smile a proof of God
And as she blossoms
like an animated star
The space between you grows
She distances in the hundreds
of ways she must

And when she leaves
You take in the breath of the world
and see out into the landscape differently
And you love her as you love the sunrise

Ishq

I undid our common ground
or was it your jack hammer?
You opened my eyes with a crowbar,
hugged me with vise grips,
drenched me with your kiss,
flashed a trick mirror on my viewpoints,
tried punching holes in my reason,
with a power drill.

Did I believe our trailing and jagged love story
should make sense, not get ugly?

Your left-field logic and hyperbolic metaphors
dizzied my mind — as you tirelessly argued
me to the mat — exhausted into — why bother?
I was no match for your wild wisdom
and mammoth energy.

But beneath your ladder and hammer,
I grasped your unbearably tender
pomegranate-heart,
leather-skinned heroism,
shielding easily bled seeds.
I shielded them too.

Your visions dragged ruin in their wake
and as life threw you wrecking balls
you hauled them up your mesa
and kept their wreckage for art,
feeling privileged for being chosen.
How could something so wrong
be so perfect?

For cheating death, you won
a three-cornered character —
Sisyphus, Zorba and Job.
But would Bucky call it a stable triangle?

Fires stripped your land,
storms collapsed your home,
wind dropped a tree on your dome.
The orchard you planted,
in the manner of Solomon,
withered and died.

Neglect and a "hard to kill" credo
weathered your bones and
your gut turned on you.
The Almighty's fist delivered you
to the emergency room, and often.
You smiled in the face of it,
arose and loved God the more.

Life's pummeling thinned your armor,
tenderized your flesh,
made way for light to breathe in —
and your love of creation grew
more verdant out of the dust.

Sometime after our amicable demolition,
out of ground zero, a slow refurbishing began —
first with expansion-joints, giving way
to spacious new additions — whole new wings —
widening my heart into expanding living rooms,
opening to gardens of poppies and sunflowers,
stinging nettle and roses, near large enough to hold
your flourishing calamitous spirit.

Meeting Risala

Just go to her
open-door house,
a warm house,
a hothouse,

What you could
expect for an orchid
arrayed in exuberance,

With iridescent petals
of scarlet and sanguine,
always at the height
of her fashion but never
concealed.

Her laughter revealing —
climbing scales of
sopranic joy — unabashed —
eyes, smiling horizons.

Seated at her hearth,
ears dangling pendants of color,
a golden fan of jeweled icons
raying out from the mantle,

a chorus of beloveds beside her,
circling like prayer beads,
chanting sacred sounds of emptiness,
sounds that fill with stillness —

This is what shapes the chalice of her heart,
the orchid-pouch which holds
the essential perfume of her Being.

From this she feeds
the hungry.

Yahrzeit

He probably had enough of this world,
locked in his tower of worries.
We thought they were too small
to take notice of, unworthy
of his concern and obsession.

We didn't understand.
His frets were trapped
in that dungeon,
with dead ancestors,
who had taken all the space,
pressed to suffocation —
they couldn't be put to rest.

He had so little sleep.

Still, there were those times,
a turret window opened,
and as if from a belfry,
out flew uncoiling streamers
and confetti,
like jack out of the box,
Pagliacci at play,
his dropped-down humor
came goading us to laughter,
and for those moments
in that light, it made sense,
our being together.

Then, there was that
unforgettable gesture,
as he lay on the gurney,
left palm to his forehead,
like someone from a silent movie
in befuddlement and blunder,
realizing the right side of his body
was paralyzed by a stroke
(as if he were to blame).

They placed him in a stationary
hospital bed behind the curtained divider.
Darkness hung outside the window.

After the pneumonia,
we silently spoke,
as if he needed permission
to bow out.
And I assured him then,
as if I knew.

He believed me.

Now, I think it wasn't only me
but those dead members speaking
to him in chorus.

"Harold, no worries.
Come away Home."

Loving Lilacs

I planted them for you —
so you could see them
from your new window.

In Spring,
I would hand you a bouquet
and you'd hold it
in your cooling hands,
half close your petal-lids
and smile a small ecstasy.

Your once well-occupied hands —
joined to a mixing bowl,
rolling pin, darning egg or iron,
smoothing timely wrinkles,
weaving the mendable holes
from what had worn thin.

It was reassuring to keep the hands going
and the radio on.

All the humming mornings of fresh intentions
and frozen orange juice, new meals
that held the non-perishable flavor
of leftovers past.

Warm pharmaceutical soups,
palliatives for ill sisters,
carousel birthday cakes
and golden domed apple pies.

And all the goods
that couldn't be swallowed,
expectations never fitting
your small bowl of joy,
riddled to a sieve by tiny agonies,
wedging their way into fragile cracks

of nearby walls, bringing you to your bed,
the comforter in need of comfort.

Your tears fastened me to your sorrow,
unable to offer my stifled love—
fearful of blame for my untrainable heart,
paused weak-kneed, defenseless —
until our needs brought you to your feet
and serving hands.

The grace of Time allowed for us,
our diverse worlds shifted,
until in your need, I brought you
into my field — to a new home,
and the vision of my garden:

"I will plant you lilacs."

"I hope I'll live to see them."

"Now they're all in bloom,
new shoots everywhere.
Can you see them?
Can you capture their scent?"

As the petitioners who offered up
burnt myrrh and frankincense,

"Can I send you today's sweet living lilacs?"

What Remains

Aunt May lay in a care-home bed,
side bars jailing any flailing motions,
the air hung tinged with antiseptic.
Her attention lay at a new frontier
beneath her translucent lids.

A once impish grin flat-lined,
communications at rest or elsewhere,
a still-life picture belying her
thousands of hours walking
or wheeling others
through hospital halls volunteering —
one of her quiet generosities.

Just then
out of her coma-like silence,
an utterance forces open her sealed lips —
a staccato of words ricochet
through the sour vacancy,

"Forget it.
Forget it. Forget it. Forget it."

Forget what? I puzzle.

"Forget it.
Forget it. Forget it."

What was being remembered
that needed forgetting?

Her long-awaiting anger
at a preoccupied father,
ex-husband, boss, herself?
The pain from her curved arthritic spine,
her burdensome life supporting
a blind mother and ill sister,
her love life too unsatisfying
to dampen the desert
of her loneliness?

"Forget it.
Forget it. Forget it."

Or was it a tic without meaning?
Why this phrase and not another?
Was it a message, a gleaning,
an offering from her fading life,
a transmission of wisdom…?

Remember to forget.

When Crows Came
For Walter

Near dusk, the grandfather cedar
outside your window was visited
by a raucous chorus of crows,
their shattering voices
an alarm.

Did you hear them
breaking through the dimming sky,
the night dropping through
to take you?

They were so harsh
and you so silent,
I wanted to push back
the night, to tell you,
not to let you go
without knowing
this truth.

Unlike the truths you fiercely held —
your gospel —
of reproducible proofs
you used to gauge
our tough and tender center,
navigating the inner chambers
of arteries and vessels —
discovering obstructions —
a doctor of the heart.

Measuring narrowing passages,
detecting with equations,
calculating numbers and formulas
for the measure of a heart.

But your life passages constricted,
and work went underground,
you paced through the hidden corridors
of your brilliant, dark and remarkable mind,
to wear out or drink away
blockages of world wrongs.
Rooted in your narrow corner,
surrounded by shelves of
well-read volumes,
a world pared down
in the winnowing of your life.

Still one trait never lessened,
quieted, yes, but remained to the end
and beyond — your loving care,
your generous reach of kindness
providing for the life around you.

Know this truth — your essence —
Your heart beyond measure.
Your heart, ever beyond measure.

You — always there,
like the cedar, that is
now no longer with us,
nor the birds.

Is that why they're called
"a murder of crows"?

FLORA

The Light of Flowers

The Madia Flower

Crepuscular flower,
coming alive
at the golden edges
of the day.

At dawn she spreads
a glow upon the ground.
I glimpse her
briefly opened eye
before she draws into
her narrow profile.

Then,
when the sun has reached
past its zenith
and I have stretched
to the limits of my day,
the curled and inconspicuous
Madia — held back in quiet cover,
during the great blaze of daylight —
unfurls her modest petals
in a dance of no hurry
to expose the remains of the sun.

This August sun
which draws me out
Into the fast-doing world,
loosens its hold
and the humble Madia,
with her golden leash
of fragrance,
guides me back
into her mild, yellow face
and red bindi dot,
brings me to the sun
of my own knowing.

Borage

Borago, robust madre
of the Mediterranean,
bristly-hair, leafy girth,
festooning the earth,
sheltering small life
under sweeping
crenelated skirts.

What is your mission?

A gathering of milk maids
nursing the riot of bee folk,
The Sisters of Pollination —
crowning luminous blue stars,
befitting of Mary?

Comforter of the solemn,
ailing-hearted,
Apothecary —
bearing tonic for courage —
alchemist, transforming
melancholics into brave hearts?

Or a miner of minerals,
pulling buried treasures
out of their long sleep,
transforming them
to new liveliness —
and storing them
deep in your pockets.

Then, falling over yourself
with widespread plenitude,
you offer us nourishment
with every part of you.

Planting Roses

To plant roses is
to bury living treasure.

Watch patiently,
the flushed red leaves
announcing each bud:
a tightly packed animated gift
imperceptibly breaking open —
a jewel come alive.

Its color, fragrance and fruit,
would be enough,
yet with a subtler glance,
it reveals an inner picture —

Unfurling petals spiraling us
into the many-layered lodgings
of our labyrinthian heart.

Queen Anne's Lace

There is no need of a palace
with a canopy that rivals
the tracery of a Renaissance
Cathedral.

If this sounds too grand
for a wildflower,
then a Chantilly parasol
blown upward by the wind,
which doesn't keep out weather
but attracts higher signals
toned from the stars.

Its beauty is these notes
come into flower,
beguiling our eyes and
inspiring our seeing —
a vision-expanding balm—
remedy for the near-sighted.

Beneath her noble stem,
an underground throne —
not wrought in gold carat
but a primeval carrot,
piercing through
the royal firma.

Psalm of the Rose

Behold the taut bud,
amassed within it,
a serene cloister of petals
in deep contemplation,
poised in prayer,
as precious substance
subtly streams through —
an inner anointing —
swelling them
in fiery concentration,
awaiting the moment
when the sun singes their seal
and they are burnt open
on the altar of their thorny spine,
unfurling their choir of petals
whose song is color's radiance,
whose emanation is incense sublime —
all a bestowal of ecstasy.

Mullein

Quiet-footed pioneer,
drifter of the raw frontier,
homesteading where few tread,
rooting through hardened clay
and stone gaps, mining minerals,
boring airways for the breathing earth.

In what appears the blink of a night,
your gentle explosion of colossal leaves —
looking as though the moon strew silver petals
in a welcoming carpet for new-seeding life.

Then, gathering forces from above and below,
till wondrously, out of your flannel footing
arises the sturdy spine of Aaron's Rod, Jacob's Staff —
a torch raying golden florets of earthed light.

Those Dahlias

I could have trellised them
when they were still young,
helped them to be upright,
stay together, keep
to their breeding,
obedient to the sun.

They're all lying around now,
independent, sinuous
stems curving suggestively
or recumbent as enchanting sirens,
pointing at us from every direction
like perfectly exploding garnets —
drawing us into their deep hubs,
like unwitting flies to a Venus-trap.

Somewhat nonchalant,
they await to be adored,
perhaps to be picked up
and taken home.

Yes, they're irresistible.
Isn't that the point of beauty,
to disarm us to the crux of our soul?

Dandelion

Intimate of the kind earth,
misunderstood friend of the grasses,
humbly dazzling in your flowering-yoke,
smelling of curled-up sun.

You break open your invisible shell
and voila! like a quick-change artist —
out comes a flock of silken plumage,
wind-propelled seeders,
stationed for creation.

Dandelion for the Young

Dandelion, pet of Thine —
shining lights for children's eyes,
for fresh bouquets of perfect size
to fit their fists and take away —
as loving gifts for mother's pay.

Chamomile Underfoot

I stepped on your loveliness,
you curbed me with an
outburst of fragrance,
my toes smiled, complicit.

I'll better watch my step.

But now, how can I ask
to give up your flowers
to offer your sedative,
for my need of sleep?

Chamomile Tea

I'd like to better know
the chamomile,
how it came to calm
what keeps each of us awake?

All the things that tumble in —
from the hard-to-digest world —
continue rumbling mind and belly,
too coarse to percolate down.

Chamomile, your nature — an antidote —
never bristly, bitter or harsh
but a notably sunny, obliging disposition —
as perfectly rested sun.

Sweetening our load with your genius,
putting out flames of bad news, insults
and onions,
mellowing to a digestive condition.

Your golden infusion,
a comforting floral milk —
refining and distilling
what heads cannot release —
settling us in —
to perfectly rested sun.

Chamomile in the Air

To put my belly on the ground
and see from a world
of minuscule seeds, at home
in this mine-stripped soil,
now aired and fed into good humus,
so their spider web roots can grab
crumbs of compost-breaded earth.

Out of broad sunlight — thin-spun threads
weave into a miniature bush of light ,
scaling the air on filament stems
branching feather-down leaves,
with a clutch of golden-satchels,
gatherings of florets,
indivisible to our eye.

If they could speak with
their tiny white tongues —
air their soft-spoken messages,
from convex-yellow mouths —
I imagine they'd tell us,

"I blossom for the earth
and all its unfastened residents."

Like This

Shall we open like the rose —
petals unfolding, reaching, or fluttering —
till they fly away — leaving only a naked heart?

A Quintet of Sunflowers

I

Who can ignore your carillon of yellow
making joyous noise to God and company?

Who could miss your tightly packed ensemble of seeds,
musically orbiting like the spheres?

II

Some half grown to my shoulder,
some look me in the face
others tower over —
irrepressible in summer,
humbling in autumn,
frozen over by winter —
sludgy spent sunshine —
robust fodder for Spring.

III

A radiant golden mane —
with wide-open center —
mouth,
eye,
navel,
heart,
womb —
all in one,
with celebration around it —
Was yellow ever so fondly revealed?

IV

They could never be posies.
These are gold-tufted giants
climbing their own beanstalks,
big-footed roots knuckling
deep in the ground.

How else could it carry that king-sized head
that mimics the sun all around.

V

Receive its light,
then reach into
its dark heart.
There's meat there,
seeds you can take hold of,
crack open with your teeth,
place in your mouth
and chew like a monk
or squirrel,
or bury for
next summer.

WRESTLINGS

Between Darkness and Light

If Each

If each one of us ate one small grain of our darkness
there wouldn't be so large a portion for the scapegoats
to swallow.

Retreat

Drop what you're doing.
Leave, before it's too late.
Get lost!

If you don't take time out
for the Real,
the Invisible may snatch you,
take you off course,
land you on your back,
put you on retreat.

A train on a track
can only follow
one direction.

There's no well-worn way
to the nameless places
where your truth lies —
the untrodden path,
hidden away by none other,
so bring a machete too!

Bound Feet

Crowns and papal tiaras
elevate the height of monarchs.
Democracies become taller
from their feet.

The Emperor whose adoration
for the tiny feet of a dancer
fell into a cultural madness—
binding the feet of small girls.

All the tender toes
bound and broken
to never run free,
sealing their destiny
of disability or decadence,
no work, no escape,
contorting flesh into
a beauty of controlled deformity,
crippled toes named lotus flowers,
erotic love handles for the masters
of the controls.

The custom, though passé,
still has ravaging tracks —
each nation according to its norms —
selling, stealing or locking girls away,
shutting their doors of learning,
forcing them to please men
or removing their organs of pleasure,
gagging hearts and choking wombs,
broken lives and gendercide,
parched earth for lotus buds.

Bridling hands and persistent boots
violate the force greater
than culture's moment,
dwarfing palaces, churches,

temples, mosques, state buildings—
cannot be buried, burned or
annihilated, here before us
and will be long after us.

She cannot be bound,
She who infuses all life,
breathes all breath,
moves through our veins,
hinder this and we lock up
our Source,
rape our mother and
eat with an empty fork,
live life in a cold, dry womb.

Bow and kiss those feet,
roots of civilization,
that carried the water,
quenched the need
carried us beneath her heart
and wove our human nest.
Her power — nature of nature.
Revere her flowers
or starve of fruit.

Jean d'Arc

Before the fatal day,

her life was predicted within a short wick of passion —

Eyes alight

Ears burning

Heart ablaze

Voice aflame

France kindled

Soldiers ignited

Horse blazing

Enemy extinguished

Faith inextinguishable

nothing but her flesh left to burn

Bridled

Rearing up, wild-maned,
kicking from your haunches
or stabled away for safety
and sanitation,
clenching teeth bridled.

What rage bites behind imprisoned jaws?

Chewing on grist that won't go down,
undigestible resentments
best coughed up,
instead spur ruminating
treadmill thoughts,
the nutrition gone.

What holds it at bay?

The reigning mind shackles escape
of sleep — chiding and self-incriminating,
tightening the raw-hide leash.
Runaway thoughts range out
to justify and blame the world —
all feeding the nag —

the centaur, driven by animal instincts
and shame of them,
tries to reconcile with the stable-person.

Turn its head, your head —
keep the nugget within it all,
then loosen the halter.

Slow down the velvet equine nostrils
forcing breath or not breathing at all,
reverse course towards mercy,
murmur sweetest names for your ear —
heart-passwords, until air consumes fire
and the bridle is whispered open.

Killing Words

Listen!
No gunfire, no explosions,
no warnings, for that matter,
but friend beware
of invisible murders.

Listen for the hidden signs,
unheard-of distortions
and manipulations
that seep into thinking,
tattoo images on your mind.

Hear the deadly assaults,
fired from mouths
of fabricators of facts,
warlocks of words,
casting spells
with repetitions
and reversals.

Watch your head,
they hurl living shards
from the Babel Tower,
surgical artillery
for lobotomies,
to weaken the will with
garbling and hedging.

It's clean violence —
no visible blood.

What remains?
Counterfeit impressions
twists of truth,
shadows of colors,
trails of hate.

"They're only words."

What are words
but sounds —
creations.

Imagine the Creator
in this devious play,
reversing reality,
turning everything
upside down.

What would we stand on,
the sky?

Above us,
clouds of stone and clay,
weighing us down,
flattening us,
no man or woman upright.

All of us on our bellies
as snakes bargaining fruit
at the tree of knowledge.

This Mind, The Mind

1. This Mind

Location:
a small planet-shaped
way-station, head-quartered
on this traveling upright body,
orbiting irregularly in its own
and other surrounding currents:
at times straight away, with
    purpose,
other times derailed from its track
    —

meandering to uncharted
watery worlds of long wavy turns,
or short staccato-like trips.

Then, not remembering
the why or where of the going,
but that something is forgotten.

1. The Mind

Locationless:
here and beyond
the destination of sunshine,
marked with planets —
spiraling banners of galaxies
orienting the firmament —
spanning the universe's
unending-huddle —
all within a limitless latitude.

Without enclosure
yet within all enclosures.

2. This Mind

A home for homeless
information,
a motherboard,
a radio headset,
receiver and network,
channeling wanted and
unwanted stations,
a trackless accumulation.

A warehouse of broken,
replaying records,
centuries of storage,
old boxes with bent lids,
stamped with tiny pictures
from foreign places,
remnants of imaginations
of a past in search of a new world.

2. The Mind

The Great Host —
housing luminous ethers,
timeless archives:
encompassing chronicles,
chromosomes, roots,
fossils and fingerprints,
grandmother neurons and synapses,
the subtlest and most impenetrable.

Abode of the Alpha and Omega,
The Logos, the Akasha.
Life encoded and available.

3. This Mind

An ark floating in its own waters,
housing shape-shifting beasts
in varying numbers:
the likes of great lumbering
lizards with thwacking tails,
quick-headed vultures
tearing their prey,
picking and chewing
at the dead of the day.

Wild cats pacing,
darting deer with fearful,
glowing eyes,
slow posing sloths,
mammoth-mouthed hippos,
feigning opossums,
and a run-away mule,
to mention some
roaming the oceanic.

3. The Mind

Womb of archetypes,
spewing and patterning
avatars, mythic origins,
spawning divine qualities
all-creating, unceasing,
collapsing and rebounding.

The zodiac of fixed stars:
celestial portals of effulgent Beings
changing their aspects
with visits from the sun.

4. This Mind

A hall of mirrors,
each one uniquely bent,
differently distorting,
through broken-off
pieces of life —
not this, not that,
customized blinders
concocting singularities,
seeming unreconcilable,
enacting scenes in parades
of paradox —

Smoky apparitions,
flashing after-images,
of magical thinking,
mirages and chimera,
all clouding the longing
for the vanished garden.

4. The Mind

No frame of mind.
No distortion,
all-seeing clarity,
hierarchies of light.

Impersonal features
of the unseeable face,
ceaselessly morphing,
re-shaping, breaking apart,
making anew
in luminous gardens.

5. This Mind

Serving a subpoena,
a scathing indictment,
a harshly lit courtroom,
a bald, barrel-chested bailiff,
a tireless prosecutor,
a tiresome defense,
a drawn-faced defendant,
a waffling judge,
a hung jury,
a half-hearted appeal,
justice imprisoned,
freedom its inmate.

5. The Mind

Truth eclipsing verdicts,
laws, dictates, commands,
tablets, scrolls, volumes,
all guidance —
sagacious or mad.

Vastness bridging poles of duality —
Justice weighing on timeless scales
of creation's unfolding balance —
the Omniscient wheel turning —
from and to the Home of Light.

6. This Mind

More than the tyranny of comparing
and appraising,
More than the cool ash of thoughts,
or heated journeys after a question mark.
More than heir to the history of longings.

A dominion beyond our knowing,
belonging to The Mind ripening within us,
all of us pregnant — minds contracting, in labor,
carrying seeds of our next birthing —
limitlessness — thrusting — crowning —
divine inheritance becoming human being.

TOWARD LEVITY

Making Light

Light Breakfast

The sun casts its light
through my bedroom blinds.
Arousing this bottom-feeding fish,
I am lured,
pulled from the ocean
of sleep.

"So soon?" I ask.
"What happened to the moon?"

"It's here—in miniature,
swallowed by the dew,
cream of the milky way.
Sip this morning brew
for today's star-steeped news."

Ears

Unlike eyes that pierce,
or mouths that purse,
brows that frown or
teeth that clench,
ears don't intimidate.
One is not threatened
by a mean ear.
At worst — one is not listened to,
or best — one is heard.

Ears range from soft, downy shells
to prominent, pop-out conches.
Genies sport a pointed version,
receive extra-terrestrial data?
Draping lobes of the Buddha
predict wisdom and longevity.

No matter age, shape or size,
all humbly receive the realm of sound
with little choice or control besides
plugs or hearing aids.

Not so in animal eardom,
which may draw back, perk,
wiggle or periscope.

Elephant ears graciously wave in slow motion,
like giant fanning palms
dismissing flies or other undesirables,
or entreating as a queen.

Deer ears entrance with alertness —
their heads without them are unimaginable!

Rabbit's distinctively upstanding ears
scope the field for their scores of pursuers.
Fennec fox's far-reaching ears hear underground!

Dolphin's aerodynamic audition needs no protrusion at all,
while bats' echolocation adjusts its hearing as desired.

Dog ears are no less than an art for the breeder
but their ancestral beginning arose from
the ingenuity for listening.

How might this world be if humans
brought as much genius to their ears
as to their tongues?

Making Soup

Golden lentils swollen from an overnight soak,
drained and poured into a stained enamel soup pot,
half filled with water.

As the beans begin to boil,
foam clouds rise to the top
and I skim — spots begin to arise.

Heat agitates the water,
shaking out the growing lentils —
more dark spots float up.

Are these spots little bugs,
who ate before me,
lived from these same lentils?
I'll have to spill it out, start over.

Not so fast, I advise myself.
I remove a steamy speck to cool.
This might be a germ or part of the hull
or some leguminous offshoot.

I pull out a pair of glasses
for further examination,
but the spot's too small.
A second pair of readers is required
on top of the first, and another
(looking like a rejected version
of a fly's composite eyes).

I can barely make out germ, seed or insect,
impressive to see how close they are
in form, like siblings or cousins,
yet an entire kingdom apart!

Aha!
I see an ever-so-small hint of departmentalization —
no legs, but a definite forming on one end,
an ever-so-tiny differentiation (with my tri-foci)
that must be a head.

Captivated by its minute elegance —
the refined form of this minuscule creature.

Momentary awe precedes another realization —
I've been captured in the primal soup of creation —
And now, I must spill mine.

Queries

If north is true, where do other directions lie?

Do stars ever taste water?

Do extroverted turtles become depressed under the
weight of their cover?

Do snowflakes sense a loss of individuality when they're
shoveled into a pile?

Do stinging nettles unnerve milkweed?

Do butterflies remember crawling on their bellies
devouring leaves?

Do shadows always turn away from the sun?

Is the rainbow a glimpse of something more?

When a question finds its answer, does it lose interest
and let go?

Is each moment a molecule of our destiny?

The Hummingbird and the Cow

Two passengers came on board this life,
each exerting a certain influence
on the shaping of my ways.

One leads with light and levity, free-flying into
the throat of every color-speaking flower,
sipping the hibiscus out of life, as it lasts,
and helicoptering onto the next red moment.

This tiring tempo chagrins my other rider,
who ballasts through life slowly nosing clover,
champing select greens, pacing time
for her quartet of stomachs.

The iridescent flyspeck has the fearlessness
of a chihuahua,
dragging the cogitator by a nose-ring,
but the unhurried one digs her hooves
and still is air-lifted away.

I stand between them,
pulled by their opposing rhythms.

One scheme to break this Gordian Knot —
become a field large enough
for flocks and herds,
where deer, rabbits, owls, eagles, foxes,
bears and lions can dwell.

A hummingbird and cow will be
unnoticeable, just two members
among a Peaceable Kingdom.

Keeping Odd Socks

Keep a place for the odd sock in the back of your drawer.
You never know when a mate will arrive —
that vanished, far-flung or misplaced other
may unexpectedly show up after you've given up hope,
return like the prodigal son.

I've often wondered why the stay-at-home son —
steadfast and dutiful — was downplayed, while the derelict
deserter was a celebrated hero,
but when my second sock was recovered,
I too was elated.
They both become usable.

Value accrues to what is lost when found,
though in time there may become holes in that.

The Rose and the Onion

If the rose and onion
exchanged wardrobes,
would the rose weep
as strong-strapping
petals peeled away?

Would she sorrow for
the loss of her musk
and myrrh breath
once lovingly sniffed
and fawned over,
turning into fumes?

Would the onion of utility-frock
feel itself a turncoat
with its newfound color —
its make-over —
from full-bodied allium
of sulfuric strength
to an underground beauty
easily dropping its supple skin?

Renaming the Frost

Who named the frost "Jack"?
Someone hasty, in a hurry,
their mind on shoveling or
chiseling the snow from the driveway.
A bit more thought would have
yielded a truer name for one with
so vast a footprint —
carpeting meadows, roof tops,
lakes, and trees in whiteness—
a nickname does not do.

A ponderous name, perhaps —
"William Warren Wutherford," for example.
William Warren Wutherford walked with wintry feet;
with winged whiteness, he whispered his name.
But this could be tiresome to children
with noses pressed against crystal-splashed windows
watching their breath glisten on the frosted panes.
They might prefer a — Phinneas Phipps.

Or how about Clarence, or Oliver Frost, or Robert?

Why not a feminine name?
(Women know how to furnish a chill when needed.)
Cross out flower names such as Iris, Gladiola, or Hyacinth.
Petunia would never do.
Now, the Lily — pristine white — does have possibility,
but associations with Easter could confuse
the seasons or mix the metaphors.
And we had best stay away from Biblical names,
which conjure images of Prophets
wandering through the desert.
The chilled earth calls for a more northern nomenclature —
Gwyneth, for example.
Gwyneth Frost — doesn't quite roll off the tongue.
Perhaps the Frost of Gwyneth.
More fit for Beowulf.

Or Helen of Frost! Too Greek.
A Russian association would be appropriate —
Snezhana, Yaroslava, or Pavlushenka,
Too unpronounceable.

And what difference does it make, anyhow?
A frost is a frost by any other name.

The Misanthropic Gardener

The downcast petal of her brim
casts a shadow, which mirrors
the southward corners of her mouth.

Most likely, it was back many hats ago
that her expression settled,
now eyes ashen and cheerless,
uninviting of human disturbance.
All, most all, is saved for the silent,
controllable splendor underfoot.

Daily she plows her smileless love
into the modest plots,
walks about her subsidiary axis
of the earth —
her orbit marked by a surprising
deliverance of beauty,
rarely missing a season's sampling
of blooms.

With protective gloves she parcels
a scoop of bagged meal,
feeding the ground between
its growth spurts.

The garden's design is rarely attentive
to height or shape or color,
a rather random placement of annual
and perennial,
maybe just convenient or democratic —
but the twin pieces of ground
(a straight, parted path down the center)
respond safely wild, slightly heedless,
always show-stoppers.

Usually ignored while crossing her path,
I might inquire about a flower or two,
comment on the beauty there,
see if I could cultivate a smile.

Once I glimpsed a moment when bougainvillea
and narcissus slipped out between her thin lips.

A Different Song

I awoke this morning to an odd sound.
Amid the congenial chorus of birds,
there was a song I never heard,
a jarring rap, tap, tap, tapping
like a small piercing metal hammer,
as if a mechanical bird,
a sound decoy, was set.
Too contrived.

Perhaps it's just a baby bird
first learning to sing.
Listening again,
yes, that's what it must be.

Distracted by my alarm…
when I return to listening,
I cannot find it.
Not even a tap.

Did some large Wagnerian Bird
with bold breast and a horn-like
feather head-dress pierce and peck at you,
to silence your tinny sound?
Like tone-deaf children who try to sing
but are intimidated
by insensitive music teachers,
then never sing again—
only mouth the words.

I can't hear my little friend at all now.
My heart descends.
I want to say,
"Sing out little bird.
Don't yield to that bully bird.
Sound your sound.
Without you all those lush voices sound—
too perfect, more a canned rendition

of bird songs.
Sing your song, like none other."

Now, I hear it!
Faint and slow.
It sounds depressed.

I want to encourage it.
"Good timing!
Well done!"
No audible response.

Maybe there is a developmental sequence
in the ripening of a song,
Ornithologists and well-seasoned birders
may scoff at this idea.
"You know nothing of bird songs. Ridiculous!"
From that I become the little tin hammer...
To them I say,
"I'll not be made small.
TAP! TAP! TAP!"

I have not heard the little bird for quite a while...

I like to think he hammered things out,
caught onto the family song,
with a full and true trilling,
almost unrecognizable amidst the choir,
perched on his nest, with proud puffed chest,
full-throated, exhilarated, with a bit of a rap.

PLACE

Placeholder of Light

Rain in the Canyon

This open-throated canyon never hoards.
The rain that falls upon it is freely passed,
wakening dormant mosses, seeds and spores,
leaving a brood of spirits in the mist.

To slow its travels, obstacles are everywhere laid,
in an ever-changing debris-strewn carpet:

Woven grasses with hardscrabble blades trap it,
mycelial threads imbibe it, weaving themselves
through tiny pores in the earth,
dips and hollows in the terrain pool it,
throngs of elfin wildflowers sip it as fresh mead.

Creatures too small for our eyes
capture their portion, quench themselves,
fattening as they guzzle,
for the unceasing work we could never do.

Changing rhythms play through its flow,
symphonic brooks, water piccolos,
digestive gurgles, rapids
shimmy and tumble —
over and again
always differently.

Before cascading to its depths,
death intervenes, ferrying broken twigs
and branches, departed logs zig-zag down,
shepherding dried leaves and fragments
of fallen life on their way to being soil.

As mother's milk fills her child and empties her load —
this earthen chalice soaks and swallows the clouds,
all appeased.

The Headlands

Remains
from the ocean's
lusty appetite —

eating away with hurling laps
and salty teeth
seizing relentlessly,
consuming boundaries,
pounding majestically

like an unceasing lover's
crushing weight,
heaving its sodden-breath spray
and deafening serenades —
leaving necklaces
of sea greens on her shore.

She, widely indifferent
yet open to such revamping,
gives herself without discretion
or restraint.

Jerusalem Stone

Only one stone is used
for the buildings in Jerusalem.

Native rock of this land,
I speak to you.

Your long-withstanding
and broken face
is everywhere here:

A face that is a crypt of
civilizations.
Your pores like eyes
squinting in the sun,
witnessing from
your dense silence.

Could the sum of
reverent visitors
and mortared prayers
know the apocalypse
petrified inside you?

You are the teeth of the skyline
speaking out in different tongues:
a ferment of sweet and hardened voices,
of calls, prayers and curses
commingling in a dissonance —
a drone of unresolved diversity.

Stone of Jerusalem,
your body — colors of flesh —
pink and white, ochre and tawny —
lifted from your calcified
underground sea, carved into bricks.

Brick upon brick,
foundation stones
upon which the Holy Temples,
churches and mosques
aspire to bridge earth to heaven.

Bring down the prophets!
I want to see them — all of them —
from posts of different times,
gathered together here
speaking in tongues of light —
hands beaming upon one another,
each giving honor to one another,
rejoicing in glorious communion
joined with echoing choirs of Hallelujah.

What is hard in us will someday
turn to stone.
What is light will rejoin the stars.

Blessings from the Garden

May you stand tall and proud
yet able to bow to the light as the sunflower
May you attract goodness as lavender attracts bees
May you climb to the heights like a pole bean
and be firmly grounded as a beet
May your friendships be as nourishing and substantial as broccoli
May you develop ever-growing layers of strength like an onion
May you pierce obstructions as a carrot pierces the earth
May your thoughts be as crisp and wholesome as an apple
May your thinking be as deep as the sage
May your mouth be as sweet and moist as a peach
May your humor be as zesty as a kumquat
and zingy as a chili pepper
May your life be as robust and abundant as zucchini
May you exude love, fragrance and beauty as a rose
And may you age well, grow in bouquet as the wine grape.

Wild Light

No corrals
fencing shadows
mountain ranges
nibbling trees
or grass grazing it

without rain bowing
mist weighing
or dust trapping it
into a sunset

free in open
groundless desert
of space
to go unbroken —
at its own speed —
beyond

kindle the ashes
of another universe

or rest
in the hidden
primordial dawn

Where Goodness Is Found

Here it is —
a small red boat,
a rosy smile bobbing on the sea,

but easily capsized
by the stunts of big fish,
or caught in the jagged archway
of a whale's Goliath mouth
opening to eat,
or swallowing the ocean.
His nature, no less than good.

The great fish provided
lodging for the Prophet Jonah,
who had run away from
what had been asked of him.

Who is not like Jonah running from God,
frightened and unworthy?
Who is not caught by some hook of hypocrisy
deep in a pocket of the belly,
or does not fall short of compassion?

Still, Jonah was chosen,
not because he had become perfect
and not for his constant faith
but for God's faith in him,
in us.

How else could we be released
into the sea of life?

To enter a trace of such faith —
Here is goodness.

FINDINGS

Towards the Light

For the Love of Gravity

Knowing when I awaken at night,
I can reach the night stand,
find the water glass still there,
my feet able to touch down
on my familiar floor, slide over
to locate slippers beside my bed,
is a comfort.

Should my mind slip away,
it's reassuring to relocate in this body,
held down. Memories are provided
a home and I'm kept in place
until I move.

Things stay put like a loyal hound,
and those I love won't fly away
as in a Marc Chagall painting.

I don't pine for outer space
or zero gravity,

but think, how rare we are
among all the legged life,
that we stand straight up,
between sky and ground,
on these better-than-any-machine legs,
walk the baffling wonder of this wild earth
touched by the rain that comes down
on all of it.

What a plan this all is
and when my day comes to leave
my ingenious housing,
when gravity releases its assuring grip,
there's plenty of time for my
less visible self to be untethered
from my miracle body,
that only God could have imagined,
when I leave for good.

The Supermarket of Beliefs

Friend, step right up and enter here —
The Supermarket of Beliefs.

Beggars, bring your shopping carts,
check out whatever you choose,
just believe you are entitled.
Shoplifters are welcome—
in this free market, no one pays!
Open your pockets wide,
don't deny yourselves.

You, devotees of disbelief,
what do you have to lose?
Don't hold back,
these beliefs are guaranteed
by the test of time.
I suggest, "No atheists in a fox hole,"
or, "a little opiate for the masses"?
Who can resist Armageddon?

Only believe what you see?
Then try more powerful lenses!
If you can't imagine,
let me offer you these:
Simultaneous realities,
the emptiness of matter,
quarks and black holes.

Too much fact to be counted?
Here — then try some miracles:
Water into blood,
water into wine,
Shangri-La and Never Land,
Heaven and Hell.
These come in many brands
and are found in different aisles.

Sample these:
gematria and tetragrammaton,
unicorns and leviathans
Mahabharata and the Ramayana
the clay which made Adam and
the rib which made Eve,
the virginity of Mary
and the lust of Lilith,
the karma of reincarnation,
transmutation and transubstantiation,
the truth of fairytales and myths,
and the liquid light of a baby's eyes.

I, for one, buy into everything:
two or more gathered,
the trinity,
the four noble truths,
the five Books of Moses,
the sixth sense,
seven heavens,
eight wonders of the world,
the 99 beautiful names,
and the Holy One.

The ever-beginning,
greatest show on earth,
billions of years,
six days out of the utterance of a word —
creatures in every shape and motion,
and humans in every color.

And please help yourself to the great traditions:
Once, ancient breezes of the East brought
whiffs of the rose held by the silent Buddha,
kicked-up dust from the chariot of Rama,
flute songs from Krishna,
fire and smoke from Sinai,
blood at Golgotha.

All these are in the air,
stirred and drawn in the breath
we breathe.
We all live downwind of one another,
and when so moved, these winds laugh —
no, howl — at our borders and fences.
Truth finds its way through
closed doors and secret handshakes.

It's all here, there's no escaping it.
Believe it or not…
So I buy it all —
What could be too much or too many
for the dark and starry trillions?
What is impossible in the vast,
timeless universe?
What is unacceptable in the
outstretched embrace of the infinite?

So I believe in it all,
and in the one who said,
"Break your beliefs on the rock of truth."
Where nothing is bought or sold.

Be Like Water

Let's be like water,
let go of brittle ways —
leave your skin upon the shine,
allow your formed clay to melt,
dissolve into clear formlessness —
ever-reforming.

Be like water,
bride of the earth,
transparent veils, laces of shimmering rivulets,
rings of liquid sapphire, emerald and amethyst,
silvery fish and weed swimming through your hair,
body tremulous, gurgling with arousal.

The World in Our Mouth

Our mouths carry memoirs,
our tongues, recollections,
wordless stories of pleasure,
hunger and longing.

Our memory buds hold
comfort from the first
sweet milk warmth
filling our mouths,
reaching down
into curling toes.

Sweetness tanging into sour,
a deeper note — aging
into curdling or fermenting —
or the tartness of an apple,
a higher octave
playing on the tongue.

Primal nostalgia from
the once-enfolding ocean
stirs hunger for salty licks,
condensed attainably
into a crystalized crunch.

Biting an unripe persimmon
yanks the waters from our mouth
leaving cheeks sunk
and tongue bewildered
from the sting of astringency.

Young palates spit out
what's hard to swallow —
age bears the clench
of bitterness that grabs
the back of our tongues.

We savor familiar tastes
of what surrounds us —
crave the comfort of flavors
and aromas of our origin.

The fruit of our geography is to ingest
and the seeds of our history are to digest.

Appetite for Beauty

We stuff our senses
as a taxidermist packs a corpse —
ears with deadening sounds,
eyes with screens of spent light,
nose with artfully purposed poisons,
bellies with lifeless bread.

Our air is laced
with the entrails of profit.

And we live cut off
from our deepest hunger,
where only the True and Real
are fine enough to penetrate
the dead pelts that cover it.

Close all the deadening doors,
though they have you by the mind.
Be brave, go barefoot inside,
feel the soil of inner-moist darkness
where life takes root.

Whatever happens next,
even if it's only a shiver
let it happen,
don't change the station.

Stay close,
watch over its moving,
unexpected changes
coming up,
a poke of a sprout.

It won't stay the same.
We are more changing weather
than reruns — so labor
in the rainstorm's weighty clouds.

Devour the nourishing singe of sun.
Buds need the tussle of seasons,
living movement for their beauty
to break open.

Unlike the Lilies

Unlike the lilies of the field —
sufficient and clothed in perfect beauty,
fragrant and fed in their firm-footed place
(as St. Francis would have us),
we humans are delivered here
naked and incomplete,
in need of feeding,
tending, sheltering
and above all loving —
all this in delicate proportion
few receive —
and yet we go on,
in our durable imperfection,
with some imbalance or another
making our singular ways
through the seasons.

Then, in the closing of life —
there is call for more tending,
when need is most grave,
as we lie bare on the altar
of our life's last offering,
exposed and entrusting
caring hands of others

As all that we called ourselves
sheds like dry petals of a cut flower
and the perishability of our body
releases its bindings of burden,
we lighten to a thinner skin,
and might glimpse at grace —

midwifing hands ushering us
to the threshold — relinquishing
our body to our inviolable spirit —
something a lily may never know.

TIME

In Light of Time

Our Sun's Song

Each morning the Sioux sing the sun into rising.
It's never assumed that because they sang
yesterday or all the days before
that the sun will remember.

The great star's radiance is poised
beneath the horizon's pillow,
waiting for its song to awaken.

Our hearts, such tiny suns,
are all the more in need
of awakening sounds of love,
each morning of our lives.

The Unwatched Night

When the sun leaves us
for the other hemisphere,
the night goes unattended.

That other, dark unruly side
may show up and join you,
wield its influence —
your will becomes willowy,
good intentions get slanted,
unclear, or take a hike,
details get dropped or lost
and you know the devil
who roams there.

You eat a little more,
drink a little more, shadowy
solicitors capture your interest,
reflect you with fun-house mirrors,
you make unspoken deals with
yourself and those others,
in the morning your tongue is thick
and your soul hungover.

Stay inside tonight, sit
by the ash-choked hearth,
sweep around and free the embers,
blow the sparks, ignite a revival.
Retrieve the day's passed-by meetings,
hidden signs with inside stories,
fireside stories — mysteries
waiting to be cracked open.
Shine firelight on them or watch
this awaiting moment —
that's never before been seen.

Shaping of Age

Those wisps of expression
that once lightly played
upon your face,
the broken smile,
quaking laugh,
winces from rebuke,
the hollow of fear and
tightening from
disappointment,
can linger,
find their grooves,
and after so many visits
make their homes there.

Stories and secrets
you keep to yourself
sculpt your body and
draw pictures on your face.

Listen,
our form is a map of our history,
a testimony that we have
smiled many smiles,
fared considerable sorrow,
responded in all the ways
body and soul could reply.

We are here to grow kind
to the strange change of face
and reorienting body,
as we love the low-bowing
moss-shrouded tree,
surrendering to the earth.

Why We Need the Sabbath

Our lives can outgrow us
with fullness
or shrink us with emptiness.

The sun is plentiful until it's gone
and then, have we any light
to show for it?
The moon is its light keeper,
hidden or full.

The Sabbath is the moon
that holds the light of our days
to shine back on our week.

Can we make a home for light
like the moon,
reach into time, recapture
what was but fell away
overlooked?

Harvest life —
behold a slower
magnifying look —
hold it up,
gaze upon it,
weigh it,
turn it over.

Enter the curved hand of the moon
holding the glow of spacious time.
Cast a soft eye on the salt pillars
behind you, melt them in
sweeter waters of mercy,
so what is held grimly in our flesh
and bones may be let go.

Become a moon
reflecting goodness
for all those who surround you,
raying the light of Sabbath back
into our world of days.

Guessing the Light

When the nature of my body
persuades a night awakening,
I feebly bargain with my sleep
and give way to what is
beyond controlling.

Dragging my reassembling body
to the edge of the bed,
rising slowly into the cave of night,
a half-blind mole
tunneling through the unseen,
hands reaching out for
the familiar.

I relieve my body's patient waiting,
sit and wonder about the unlit time
and the procession of darkness.
Giving homage to its secrecy,
I venture to guess the hour
from its tones and shade.

From the first gray veils of dusk into
the cast of dense smokiness,
midnight's gradual concealment,
then depths of shade,
where the Greeks passed over.

The moments of near-perfect
darkness at 2:00,
the impenetrable mask
making the moon invisible
at 3:00 am,
when the hidden mystical light
might be glimpsed
before I fade back
into that other world …
disappearing from my body
into the dark of sleep.

ABOUT THE AUTHOR

As a poet, retired psychotherapist, gardener and artist, Una Kobrin's poetry traverses the inner and outer landscape, where all is included in the realm of intimate relationship. Originally from Chicago, the last 40 years Una has been a Californian, bi-located in Berkeley with her late husband, as well as living outside Nevada City, in the Motherlode of Northern California. The land was stripped of top soil during the generations of gold-mining that occurred there. Kobrin practices sacred agriculture in conversation with the earth and the individuality of the land that surrounds her. This land has been loved and recast as a canvas for diverse cultivated gardens neighboring its wild periphery, where presences often speak through her poetry. This 32-acre sanctuary, Heartstone, is home to Una and a small community of residents and working friends. She also regularly visits her daughter, son-in-law and grandchildren on the East Coast. Visit her website: www.unakobrin.com